THORNS ON THE ROSE

Western Poetry

Second Edition

John D. Nesbitt

THORNS ON THE ROSE

ISBN-13: 978-1799149316
Copyright © 2013 John D. Nesbitt
Second edition copyright © 2019 John D. Nesbitt
Author photo by: Jennifer Smith-Mayo
Cover Design by: Laura Shinn Designs
http://laurashinn.yolasite.com

Second edition published by RR Productions, Torrington, Wyoming

Licensing Notes

All rights reserved under U.S. and International copyright law. This book may not be copied, scanned, digitally reproduced, or printed for re-sale, may not be uploaded on shareware or free sites, or used in any manner except the quoting of brief excerpts for the purpose of reviews, promotions, or articles without the express written permission of the author and/or publisher.

THORNS ON THE ROSE is a work of fictional western poetry. Similarities of characters or names used within to any person – past, present, or future – are coincidental except where actual historical characters are purposely interwoven.

Dedication

For Gaydell Collier, who encouraged and inspired so many writers.

CONTENTS

PART I: DOING BETTER — 7
Like All the Others — 8
Friday's Impression — 9
Wild Rose of Wyoming — 10
Early Spring Ride — 11
When Life Is Better Than a Good Cowboy Song — 12
Labor of Love — 14
I Planted Apple Trees — 15
Held It All Together For So Long — 16
Some Things I Kept — 17
Doing Better — 18

PART II: SOME VOICES, SOME NIGHTS — 19
I Won't Live in L.A. — 20
In the Broncho Bar — 21
To Officer Miller — 22
Dark House, Dark Lady — 23
A Son and a Father — 25
In the Trails End Saloon — 26
Under Cloak of Night — 27
Palenque Chihuahua — 28
Prairie Center — 31

PART III: SONGS 37
Roasting a Goose 38
Anvils from the Sky 39
Till The Death of My Honky-Tonk Heart 40
Boss of the Bottomline Ranch 42
To the North of Old Cheyenne 44
Down in Santa Fe 46
Girls of Chihuahua 48
Jack O'Malley 50
Way Out On the Elsinore Grand 52
Jim Weston Isn't Dead 54
Nebraska Girl 57
Please Come To Wyoming 58
Lonesome Jim 60
Old Rope Corral 62
Rangeland Lament 64
Lone Winter 66
Traveler in the Snow 68
Blue Horse Mesa 70
Don't Be a Stranger 73
Great Lonesome 77
Thorns on the Rose 80
Angelique; or, A Lover's Quest 84

ACKNOWLEDGEMENTS 93

ABOUT THE AUTHOR 96

PART I:

DOING BETTER

Like All the Others

When the morning light no longer casts a shadow
From a flannel shoulder on your side of the bed,
When there's room for all my shoes and shirts and
    jackets
And I'm free to park my car up in the drive,
When the squeaking front-door hinge is answered
By the cat you never used to let inside,
When the garbage doesn't fill up half as often,
And a chicken lasts me three nights in a row—
When that's the glamor of my dawn-to-dusk,
You bet your buttons I hit the honky-tonks
To drink more than I wanted but then want
To drink one more, buy one for the lady there;
Alone, this night like all the others, I
Go home to meet the cat and sleep till dawn.

Friday's Impression

Now homeward, having left you at your door,
I sang a happy song, waved to the cops
Who lay in wait for the Broncho Bar to close.
Back on the rutted road my headlights danced
Across the snowfield as I sang my song.

Snowflakes on my hat in a world still young—
Your footprints from the front porch to the
    driveway,
Pressed lightly into Friday evening's snow,
Were covered now with Saturday like a child.

Wild Rose of Wyoming

Wyoming plains, green-silver sage on grass,
In spring the mildest, with tornadoes, hail,
Dull rattlesnakes slow basking in the sun—
Home of the cactus flower, yellow silk,
Upgrown from dust of buffalo and dreams.
When yucca stalks hang pods of fleshy grey,
Wild roses in the cutbank bloom serene,
Wild roses pink in reticence, fine-thorned.

Now winter shrouds the cactus and the sage.
Close like the badger in his den, we draw
Unto ourselves, hold in the way we feel.
But there will come a spring, and with it, hope—
The earth will warm, the roots will drink again;
Our friendship, like the quiet rose, will bloom.

THORNS ON THE ROSE

Early Spring Ride

As snow-melt spring slips happy early March,
Beneath the prairie saffron grey and tan,
Last summer's growth soft waving in spring's
 breath,
New grass smiles green. My pony wants to run.

Slowed down from lope to walk, his breathing
 even,
We listen to the saddle leather creak.
The shedding sorrel hair lifts in the breeze
To lighten in the sun and drift away.

Now all the world is growing gentle warm.
Light wind upon my sleeve reminds me of
Your fingertips, your words that touch me soft,
That turn me like the prairie grey to green.

Back at the hitching rail I rub him down,
A burlap thanks, a coffee can of grain.
Near lilac bushes budding lavender,
I see the extra saddle in my shed.

When Life Is Better Than a Good Cowboy Song

The rind I cut from around the edge
Of my pan-fried antelope chops
Goes out the back door to my dog.

Early spring evening, cool and warm,
Alone on my porch, with my boots off,
I listen to "Sioux City Sue,"
Watch sunset clouds bloom lilac,
Eat an apple and think of you.

Hatless in dusk,
Sock-footed and hand forward,
I walk to the pasture gate.
At my call he comes on a gallop,
My pony, white-stockinged in twilight,
Who has learned that the core is for him.

My hand sticky from apple juice,
Moist from the horse's nibble—
That, and that only, in the empty evening air,
Until Gene Autry's song comes playing back.
Sioux City Sue,
Sioux City Sue,
Your hair is red, your eyes are blue,
I'd swap my horse and dog for you.

THORNS ON THE ROSE

Back on the porch it hits me—
Nebraska cowboy in the song
Has it wrong.
Love doesn't call for trade-offs.
Sam gets the scraps,
Sonny Boy gets the core,
And everything I really have to offer
Goes to you.

Labor of Love

Come summer, the shadow of the power pole
Will cross the driveway as the sun moves north
To lengthen lingering days and warm the soil,
Brown blanket now, this slumbering stretch of earth.
Moved by my shovel, yielding to the hoe,
The quickened ground will bear my gifts for you—
From peas to pumpkins, peppers in a row
Like pretty maids, and mounds of honeydew.
Aware that love's not measured like the dirt,
By furrow width and shovel handle length
Or trowel depth, I wanted all the same
To fence it in with flowers, give a name
To sweat and creaking shovel, slow brute strength,
And bright red blossoms rippling like a shirt.

I Planted Apple Trees

I planted apple trees the week we met,
Trees young and supple, bending in the wind,
Now rooted on the hillside looking south.
I dream of days when you and I as one
Walk hand in hand at apple-picking time.
I'll tend those trees myself when you have gone,
And in the deep of winter, arms outstretched
Like dormant living branches, I'll face south
And know you're with me in our apple trees.

I Held It All Together For So Long

I held it all together for so long,
Carried it like a satchel of figurines,
Held on, hoping not to lose the grip
On memories I'd invested:

A pitchfork balanced on my finger tip,
To show you how I thought we'd manage life
When it came into our hands, with time.

Pincushion cactus in a dish,
To bloom at your place when they bloomed at
    mine
And keep the current flowing across the miles.

A blanket by the river, free as air,
A wicker basket, flowers in a jar,
A roadside picnic bench, an uncut pie,
Two coffee cups, and one car headed south.

As if to hold these images in mind
Would keep our love alive, I clutched them all,
Along with

A key chain, with a brass and ivory plate,
That went to places where it had no use—
California, Spain, and Mexico—
Two quail etched on an oval field,
A pair, like you and me the night
I unwrapped it in Cheyenne.

Some Things I Kept

I mopped the floor with the checkered shirt.
It didn't fit so well as time went on,
Took on a funny feel, until one day
I lopped off the buttons and the sleeves
And made a rag of what had been a gift.

Another day while I was burning things,
Just cleaning up some odds and ends,
I took the straw hat from the bedroom wall
And pitched it in the flames with the other one,
The one I'd worn out in the years between.
They both burned well, burned down to wire
    loops,
The brims, you know—you couldn't tell them
    apart.

Some things I kept: bare walls and empty rooms,
An oval bathtub big enough for two,
The quail and key chain that I carry still,
And a brass door knocker, the horseshoe holding
    luck,
Stored in a kitchen drawer beneath the phone.

Doing Better

I thought,
If I'm going to drag it by myself,
There are some parts I can do without.
As the sun went down I washed my hands with
    snow,
Cut off the head and lower legs,
Trussed the front quarters with my drag rope,
And bent against the weight.

Here at this window where so many days
I watched the winter sunsets, grew sick
With worry, waited for your call,
I see the snow again.

Here's how I'll do it now:
I'll come back and get the horse,
Wrap a rope around the legs and antlers,
Face the horse right at it, climb aboard,
Dally the rope around the saddle horn,
And head back to the empty house.

PART II:

SOME VOICES, SOME NIGHTS

I Won't Live in L.A.

I left L.A. in '71,
Headed my car up 101,
Flopped down the top and stepped on the gas,
And sang, "*L.A. can kiss my ass.*"
I made a pledge that warm spring day,
That I won't live in L.A.

I've lived in places that would curl your hair,
Places that cockroaches won't even share—
Slept in the car and in labor camps,
Salvation Army with bums and tramps,
Hotels for two or three dollars a day—
But I won't live in L.A.

Far from the land of fruit and gold
I'll stay right here with the wind and cold.
I'll scrape my windshield at forty below,
Wear double gloves while I shovel snow,
And wear long-johns from June till May—
But I won't live in L.A.

I'll live out here on the wind-swept plains
In a mobile home with rattling panes.
I'll eat antelope, drink cheap red wine,
Hit the Broncho Bar at half past nine,
Work another year at last year's pay,
But I won't live in L.A.

In the Broncho Bar

Landscape in the Broncho Bar

As she leaned to shoot the five ball,
Her pendant breast on one side
And her rib cage on the other
Described an arc.
Beyond, the green felt of the table,
Bounded by the sky-blue of her T-shirt,
Reminded me, as I set my bottle down,
Of the summer-green hills of eastern Wyoming.

Wildlife in the Broncho Bar

Wyoming cowgirl told me this one.
Pulled her Wrangler pockets inside out,
To look like bunny ears.
Said, smiling, beneath the six-point elk,
"Kiss the bunny on the nose."
Big Wonderful Wyoming, land of
Mountains, sagebrush plains, and bunnies.

To Officer Miller

Lost somewhere between the n and r,
My Chevy cast adrift on Route 16,
The white line hard to follow,
I saw your warm red beacon in the mists.

Seasick on the tilting asphalt deck
I wobbled toe to toe
And couldn't touch my nose.

And you, sad captain, took me to a safe harbor,
Dropped my anchor for the night,
Assured me more than once
You were just doing your job.

THORNS ON THE ROSE

Dark House, Dark Lady

Dark house, by which once more I stand
In grey of autumn night,
Warm from my walk along the fallow fields,
Along the lanes that she and I had known—
Dark house, faint-frosted in the moonlight,
Sits on the prairie's edge against the elms.

Two days before first autumn's frost,
Two years before this night,
Beyond those panes that now throw back the
  moon,
I learned that there were men and there were
  boys.

Dark lady, young in years, in spirit
Old as me, the man who had been a boy,
Who brought the horses saddled to her door.
Across the hayfields, down along the creek,
We rode and laughed, made love in shadowed leaf,
Listened to the voices of the corn.

Dark lady young and old who lived alone,
Young as the meadowlark in dewy grass,
Old as the coyote call that we both knew.
When wagon wheels stood frozen in their ruts,
Within the warm-lit house I poured the wine;
She played the piano, dark eyes upon the page,
Dark hair upcurled to touch the cheekbone,
Down-swirled to touch the field of bosom wool.

Tonight, beyond the darkened windows,
Beyond the elms beyond the empty house,
Across the plains, beneath the city lights
She sits at dinner with a younger man,
Older than the boys who courted her.

If she were here and saw me standing now,
What would she see? The grey upon my temple,
The ash that crumbles from my cigarette,
The red and black that cry within me as
I turn and walk away beneath the moon?

A Son and a Father

He could have been a butcher, stayed inside,
But he worked his life beneath the open sky
Alone behind the plow behind the horse.
The earth he understood—what grew from dirt,
What lived beneath, what walked and flew above.
When frost and snowfall brought his crops to rest,
His eyes turned skyward to the sound of geese.
By evening's fire he picked the grouse and quail,
Skinned cottontail and squirrel, honed his knife.
He could have been a butcher, for he knew
Each part, each joint, their secrets every one.
With duck or deer, his hands worked by
    themselves,
The knife unfailing and the meat stacked neat
As cordwood for my mother, whom he loved.
His talents were not mine; I had my own.
He taught me things a man should show a son,
Then paid my music lessons, bought my books,
And took my mom to France before he died.
"Respect your dad," my mother used to say.
I wondered if he knew as well as she
(Or I) did that I'd have to meet him first.

In the Trails End Saloon

An old man by some standards,
Seventy years in his greyish-green eyes,
A faraway tone to his wind-swept skin,
Like his sand-colored Stetson,
Cured by campfires, sagebrush, and prairie sun.
Old hands that held pitchforks and shovels,
Axes, rifles, and bridle reins
Now hold a cue stick and a glass of draft.
He taps the end of the stick on the floor
And smiling, delivers his lines.

"This cannot happen.
Even though I am old,
And the muscles in my arms have gone slack,
I will take up my spear and shield
And will help drive the enemy back to their ships,
To take their dead and their wounded
Across the water they sailed
In order to ruin our peace."

I imagine the sun and wind on his face
As he settles his sights on an antelope
Or reins his horse on the rangeland,
Kindred spirit of Archílochus and Anácreon,
Far away from any wine-dark sea
But beneath the same sun and arching sky,
Poems and tunes running through his mind,
Remembered from some distant youth
Or made up new in the shadow of the hawk,
Bringing a smile, as now,
When he holds the cue stick upright like a spear.

Under Cloak of Night

Not the bare deed itself but having done it
Is the main feature of these dreams—
The dead man underground or stowed away,
Beyond the struggle and the screams.

I'd never kill a man by light of day,
But under cover of the night
I've bludgeoned men who did no wrong to me,
And then I've buried them from sight.

But out of sight is not quite out of mind.
Our hidden guilt will rise again:
A poorly buried, nameless senseless corpse
Will surface from beneath our ken.

Perhaps thick-browed three thousand years ago
I swung a heavy shepherd's crook,
Dropped a man where he trespassed on my field,
And never gave a backward look.

Or a hundred years ago with bulging arms
I held a crowbar, steel and slick,
Paused briefly to take aim, then brought it down
Upon his shoulders and his neck.

Perhaps again I never killed a man
Except in shadowed fields of sleep,
Where acts of dread irrevocably done
Come upward drifting from the deep.

Palenque Chihuahua

At a little after midnight,
Into the hard-packed lime-lined pit
Where seven roosters had died that night,
Vicente Fernández, the pride of Mexico,
Stepped lightly as five thousand people stood
    cheering.

Down in the center of the Palenque
The mariachi sat, their chairs in a horseshoe,
While Vicente, with *sombrero de charro*
And matching outfit complete with *pistola*,
A well-built man with a full head of hair
As dark as his close-trimmed mustache,
Still in his prime at sixty,
Sang for the people he loved and who loved him.

Who loved him? The beautiful girls of Chihuahua
Who came to the ringside in throngs with roses
And hugs and kisses for Vicente, who sang
As they whispered in his ear, took pictures,
Gave messages written on napkins—to one,
A girl of eighteen, he gave his white bow tie.

Who loved him? A whispering girl's grandmother,
Out for her seventy-first birthday,
Who was brought into the ring with Vicente.
With his arm around her he sang, with the crowd,
The birthday song, *Las mañanitas*, and we knew
That he loved all the mothers and grandmothers
    too.

THORNS ON THE ROSE

Who loved him? The men who handed him brandy
In bottles they'd bought for refreshment,
Which Vicente in friendship held aloft at arm's
    length
And poured a stream into his mouth, between
    verses.
He drank many times. As I was told later,
Vicente siempre termina borracho.

Who loved him? The men who threw him their
    hats,
Who took a puff from his cigarette,
Who ushered their wives and their daughters to
    ringside,
Who could say they shook hands with Vicente.

Who loved him? Perhaps most of all
The ten-year-old girl
Who clung to Vicente and cried as she kissed him,
Cried as he took off his ornate sombrero,
Called for a pen and inscribed on the brim
A long dedication. The mariachi played on.
Later, though half-drunk or more, he noticed
She was wearing the hat backwards, so he
    switched it.

That little girl's life will forever be changed
From the night she danced with Vicente
And carried away the sombrero
With the message he wrote on the brim
As he knelt with the hat upside down on his lap
And she stood in the sand where the roosters had
    bled,

While five thousand people applauded.

Some came to sell cigarettes and drinks,
Others to bet and take bets on the roosters,
But anyone there that night could have felt
Our lives were richer from a night at the Palenque
With Vicente and all of the people who loved him.

THORNS ON THE ROSE

Prairie Center

Oasis of life in a land where death abounds,
Bosom of the plains country, this sea of grass,
Where the silver fluting song of the meadowlark
Gives way at dusk to the haunting call of the owl
And the wail of coyotes quavering on thin air.

Vast waves of earth, rumpling away for miles,
Where ants and beetles, gophers and prairie dogs,
Rattlesnakes, and badgers all live beneath the
    crust.

Where overhead, in a sky so clear and blue
That a boy lying on a haystack has no sense
Of cities and machines, money, hate, or years—
Just a sky stretching forever, across time,
Here in a land where roundup wagons rolled,
And Crazy Horse watched from a hill as bison
    grazed.

Above the boy on the haystack, flapping wings,
A snake trailing from the claws of a hawk,
A golden moment of summer that never dies
As he grows into this world so spare but rich,
Where antelope come back in numbers every year,
Dark eyes, tan coats, white flashing rumps and
    bellies
As they wheel and run and turn, linking the years,
Joining the boy on the haystack with the white-
    haired man
Who has walked this land and ridden it, mourned
    its losses,
And known it as the center of the earth.

Where every life has a story, from hopes and
    dreams
To the way things turned out to be. A young man,
    a horseman,
Rose up and hit the teacher in the country school,
Went on to work for the railroad, drove a cattle
    truck,
His face turned florid, swollen cheeks, purple
    veins,
Smoke-tinted glasses, cloudy eyes, his days of
    work
Long in the past, living in a rental house,
Remembering horses, smoking his last cigarette.

All stories end, but for the boy on the haystack,
All stories are always taking place, never ending—
His first deer, antlers glinting in the sun
As scarlet dawn gives way to yellow sky,
Walks out upon the hayfield, stops and turns.
His first horse, a sorrel with a narrow blaze
And two white socks, waits for him in the corral.

The hawk is always carrying the snake,
The young man is always punching the teacher
And thinking of the horses he used to ride.
The land and the sky and time all stretch forever
Here in this world of grass and distant buttes,

Where deer walk down through clefts too narrow
    for cows,
Browsing in the shade of ancient sandstone walls,
Leaving their heart-shaped footprints in the sand.

THORNS ON THE ROSE

Where a coyote pads along, past weathered bones,
Looks backward over his shoulder, never trusting,
Then moves ahead, his tail streaming out behind
As he trots in the phantom light of setting sun.

Where a rabbit crouches in the shade of sage,
Watching for the hawk's shadow, his sense of fate
Ingrained upon his mind from ages past,
As he holds still in the heat of noon, ears flat,
Then bolts away at the footfall of a horse.

Where antelope drift among cows to drink
From a stock tank as the windmill creaks and
    whirs
And through the clear water, clean and
    undisturbed,
The skull and bones of birds lie in the silt.

Where chokecherry bushes grow in draws and
    canyons,
Offering thin shade in summer for drowsy cows,
The small black fruit in August, when starlings
    come,
And faint red leaves for the early sign of fall.

Where grasshoppers click their wings and soar
    away
As the boy from the haystack, now in middle age,
Feels through the soles of his boots the heated
    earth
As he walks across the field and counts the bales,
Not the square bales that made a flat-topped stack
Where a boy could loll and dream on summer
    days,

But large, round hulks that dot the land for miles,
Serve well as windbreak for a mobile home
Or a perch for barnyard cats in morning sun.

Back in his pickup, he rumbles on in dust,
Where antelope cross the road in single file,
Ignore the roadside cross in memory
Of a young ranch wife who hit loose gravel and
    rolled
On a sunny day as cows looked up from grazing
And meadowlarks stopped their singing in mid-
    note.

Where a pair of Kansas hunters doze in a pickup
Parked on a warm October afternoon
Outside the two-story country schoolhouse
Where coats still hang in the cloak room, and
    blackboards wait
Some fifteen years since children's laughter rang.

Where a man on a tarp-covered haystack slipped
On an empty spot where he thought a bale should
    be,
And he slid off into space—not far, but enough
To change his life, so that he thought no more
About cows and hay, but about his neck brace,
And how he'd built a ranch to come to this.

Where a man tethered to his oxygen tank
Looks out the window and enjoys what's left,
Knowing he will never ride his horse again,
Thinking of the best way to give away his guns,
Hoping to hear the sandhill cranes once more.

The boy from the haystack, now white-haired,
    gears down

THORNS ON THE ROSE

As he turns the corner by the schoolhouse, drives
    two miles,
Where Angus cows seek the shade of a railroad
    trestle,
Where a tall, heavy man he knew, past middle
    age,
Drove forty miles from town to end it all.

He turns around at the trestle, counts the cows,
And heading west again, can't shake the thought
Of a rope around the neck, snugged to a beam,
And a body hanging for the world to see.

Better to think of other times, when things went
    well,
Like the stretch of years in his own mobile home,
A hay-bale windbreak on the west, his horse
    corral
On the east, for Pal to catch the morning sun.
All the windows open in the summertime,
Old western music on the stereo,
A slice of antelope sausage with the eggs,
And a jar of chokecherry jelly for the toast.
A sense of years to come, enough, perhaps,
To meet a woman whose ideas fit his.

Or another time, October, when a buck climbed
    up
From the mists of a canyon, found a level path,
His antlers high as he walked through fog,
    appearing,
And the boy from the haystack, now a man,
    crouched
Behind a sandstone boulder, beside a bluff,
Where the crash of the rifle echoed along the
    rocks.

Or one fading November day, hunting alone,
Waiting for the lead deer to jump the fence
Between dry pastureland and sweet corn stalks,
One good shot, piercing the thin, cold air,
And a deer laid out at the edge of the stubble,
Heat rising from a small red hole at dusk.

All stories end, even when they last forever,
Like the woman he used to meet on prairie nights
In the gun-rack bench-seat saddle-blanket cab
Where every minute counted and time stood still
Until their time was up, and left alone,
His engine silent, a cold, dark sky above,
He watched her taillights blink and disappear.

PART III:

SONGS

Roasting a Goose

You can have your fried bacon and sausage,
The best that a farm can produce—
But give me a fat-cracklin' gander,
For there's nothing like roasting a goose.

Roasting a goose, roasting a goose,
There's nothing like roasting a goose.

You can have your fine wines and Scotch whisky,
Your gin and your grenadine juice—
Just give me a bottle of red-eye,
To drink while I'm roasting my goose.

Roasting a goose, roasting a goose,
There's nothing like roasting a goose.

You can have all the lobster and codfish,
Your steaks from the elk and the moose—
For me it's a far greater pleasure
To savor a fat roasted goose.

Roasting a goose, roasting a goose,
There's nothing like roasting a goose.

And after the banquet is over,
My napkin will be hanging loose.
My chin will be shiny and greasy,
For there's nothing like roasting a goose.

Roasting a goose, roasting a goose,
There's nothing like roasting a goose.

Anvils from the Sky

She used to call me darlin'
Now she don't call me anymore.
My dreams are like old letters
Scattered all across the floor.

Our love is just a memory
When my hopes were soaring high,
For all my dreams have fallen
Like anvils from the sky.

Like daffodils in April,
Bursting out from dormancy—
Or doves in spring returning—
So I thought our love would be.

But puncture vines and sand burrs
Crept along the ground instead,
And buzzards at the roadkill
Showed me all my hopes were dead.

Now strewn across the prairie
Where the carpet flowers die,
My lifeless dreams have fallen
Like anvils from the sky.

John D. Nesbitt

Till the Death of My Honky-Tonk Heart

Though she told me she'd love me till she took her
  last breath,
All her pledges proved empty, and alone I was left
In my sadness to ponder how to make a new
  start—
And in spite of my grieving,
I would keep on believing
In love—till the death of my honky-tonk heart.

Well, I can't count the times that I watched the
  snow fall
And I heard the slow ticking of the clock on the
  wall,
And the phone never rang as the evening went
  dark—
And I waited in anguish,
Reaching deep down to vanquish
Despair—till the death of my honky-tonk heart.

And I can't count the times when alone in my car
I stared at the headlights that glimmered from
  afar,
And I wondered if the next pair would stop where I
  parked—
Though my hopes were diminished,
I would never be finished
With love—till the death of my honky-tonk heart.

Then I went to the barrooms though I know love's
  not there,
And I sang with the jukebox of love true and fair.
And I danced with the darlings of love's
  counterpart—
I forsook false romances

THORNS ON THE ROSE

And took back my chances
To live—till the death of my honky-tonk heart.

Now I'll pull things together and call up my pride,
Sing a song to my horse as we go for a ride,
Say to hell with that woman who tore me apart—
Let the old flame go under,
Search again for the wonder
Of love—till the death of my honky-tonk heart.

Boss of the Bottomline Ranch

He's a little too soft for a cowboy,
His face like a plucked Christmas goose,
A three-minute egg for a belly,
And shoulders that slope like a roof.

With a suit like a Methodist preacher's
And a buckle as big as a plate,
He cuts a fine figure at roundup,
In shoes that are flat as a slate.

He walks like a duck with a backache,
Or a hen with an egg that got stuck,
But he smiles like a cat eating liver,
Content as a pig in the muck.

For he's not your average cowboy,
And he'll let you all know he's not dumb—
He's smarter than all of you punchers,
For he's got this ranch under his thumb.

He talks about pigs and their acorns
To explain economics and chance—
"A bushel of corn is a bushel"
Is his motto for running the ranch.

When the punchers are out on the roundup,
They marvel at things they must do—
File reports on each bull-calf and heifer,
And count every yearling as two.

THORNS ON THE ROSE

Each puncher in turn duly pledges
Not one drop of drink did he take,
And the chuckwagon cook keeps a tally
Of each flapjack, biscuit, and steak.

Oh, he's not your average cowboy,
And he'll let you all know he's not dumb—
He's smarter than all of you punchers,
For he's got this ranch under his thumb.

He's got a great plan for the future,
For the cattle he says there will be—
New barns and corrals with brass hinges,
And a crew as content as can be.

Now it's true that some folks aren't unhappy,
They say things are going just fine—
The straw boss, the ranch gals and brownies,
Who meet every Tuesday at nine.

Now meanwhile the rest of the punchers
Go out as they did in years past.
They ride and check fence and at noontime
Make fun of this pain in the ass.

No, he's not your average cowboy,
And he'll let you all know he's not dumb—
He's smarter than all of you punchers,
For he's got this ranch under his thumb.

To the North of Old Cheyenne

On the plains of wide Wyoming
To the north of old Cheyenne,
On her homestead on the prairie
Lives my sweetheart Maryanne.

On a sunny summer morning
You can see my blue-eyed gal
Out among the cactus blossoms
On her buckskin horse named Pal.

For she loves to ride the rangeland
Just as much as any man—
Through the wind and sun and sagebrush
Of that wide and open land.

I recall the day I left her
Standing there with reins in hand,
As I left to seek my fortune
In the world beyond Cheyenne.

With her lower lip a-trembling
And in each blue eye a tear,
She assured me that she loved me
And that she would wait one year.

Full of hope and young ambition
I went out upon the world,
Sure that well within a twelvemonth
I'd be back to see my girl.

But the world has tricks and teases
For a lad of twenty-one,
And I soon lost all my money,
Plus my saddle, horse, and gun.

THORNS ON THE ROSE

And I found myself a-groveling
In a world of men uncouth,
Far away from wide Wyoming
And the pastures of my youth.

Now there's singing in the parlor,
Jolly songs and bawdy tunes,
As I fill the ladies' glasses
And I polish the spittoons.

Day by day I hoard my pennies
As by night I earn my pay,
Hoping soon to have the money
That will set me on my way.

For the time is drawing nearer,
As eleven months have passed
And I long to travel northward
To my prairie home at last,

Where I hope to be united
With my sweetheart Maryanne
On the plains of wide Wyoming
To the north of old Cheyenne.

Down in Santa Fe

I have seen the blonde-haired lasses
With their eyes of sparkling blue,
And I've heard the sweet love stories
Of the brown-haired maidens, too—

But of all the lovely women
That I've met along the way,
Not a one can match Ramona
Who lives down in Santa Fe.

With her eyes as black as cherries
And her lips of ruby red,
And her flowing raven tresses
Just as soft as satin thread,

She can make my heartbeat quicken
When she turns her gaze my way,
And I know there's true enchantment
In the town of Santa Fe.

I recall the day I met her
On a sunny day in June;
I was sitting in the plaza
In the early afternoon.

'Midst the tolling of the churchbells
Calling sinners all to pray,
She came walking through the pigeons
There in downtown Santa Fe.

In a dark grey dress of cotton,
And a shawl upon her head,
She had both hands on her prayer book
And her gaze fixed straight ahead.

THORNS ON THE ROSE

Just one look made all the difference
As she turned and smiled my way,
And I would have died there gladly
On the ground in Santa Fe,

But my heart went on a-beating
As the shawl and dress passed by,
And within I felt a summons
That my soul could not deny.

So I softly rose and followed
That young woman dressed in grey,
As the churchbells in the plaza
Sang a song for Santa Fe.

At the door I stood and waited
Till she came back out and smiled,
And I asked if she would like to
Sit and talk with me a while.

Then began a fond acquaintance
Which grew stronger by the day.
Now my heart beats for Ramona
Who lives down in Santa Fe.

Girls of Chihuahua

While the girls of Nebraska are clear-eyed and
 pretty,
And the girls of Montana are beautiful too,
And the girls of Wyoming are fair-haired and
 friendly,
The girls of Chihuahua are tender and true.

Esperanza, María, Ramona, Emilia,
Adriana, Faustina, Elena, Raquel,
Leonora, Milena, Lucía, Anita,
Adelita, Dolores, Pilar, Isabel.

Yes, the girls of Chihuahua are dark-haired and
 lovely,
In the ranches and pueblos where the summers
 are long—
In the cool dusty shadows of Rancho Alegre
They stroll in the courtyard and sing this sad
 song:

Por favor, vida, dame lo que me quitaron,
Por favor, vida, dame la última flor.
Por favor, vida, dame lo que me quitaron,
Por favor, vida, dame la perla de amor.

From the border with Texas to the far western
 mountains,
From Nuevo Casas Grandes on south to Parral,
From the great modern cities to the huts of adobe,
The girls of Chihuahua are true one and all.

Esperanza, María, Ramona, Emilia,
Adriana, Faustina, Elena, Raquel,
Leonora, Milena, Lucía, Anita,

THORNS ON THE ROSE

Adelita, Dolores, Pilar, Isabel.

Oh, the girls of Chihuahua are dark-haired and
 lovely,
And the girls of Chihuahua are tender and true.
Yes, the girls of Chihuahua are dark-haired and
 lovely,
And the girls of Chihuahua are tender and true.

Jack O'Malley

He was once an honest puncher
Who plied the cowboy's trade,
He rode the plains and mountains
Until one day he strayed.

His name was Jack O'Malley,
And at an early age
He fell in with bad companions
And robbed the Cheyenne stage.

His partners Pogue and Henry
Laid out a simple plan—
They said they had fast horses
But needed one more man.

With Jack to hold the horses
Out in the scrub and sage,
At Cheyenne River crossing
They'd stop the southbound stage.

The Tuesday coach from Deadwood
Came rattling through the rocks
When Pogue and Henry stopped it
And cried, "Throw down the box!"

The stage, now running lighter,
Rolled south toward Robbers' Roost
While Pogue and Henry hustled
To divvy up the loot.

Then mounted on their horses,
They passed the bottle 'round.
But before they got to Deadwood,
Jack's partners shot him down.

THORNS ON THE ROSE

Sprawled in the dust and dying,
He watched them ride away.
With failing words he whispered,
"For this I hope you pay."

His blood was spent, but justice
Prevailed in its own way.
Pogue died in a hail of bullets
Out Rapid City way,

While Henry rode to the Badlands,
And in the August heat
His horse gave out beneath him,
And left him for buzzard meat.

Now here's to all you punchers,
Keep pointed straight ahead;
Don't stray like Jack O'Malley,
Whose partners shot him dead.

To enjoy your life in the saddle
And live past middle age,
Don't be like Jack O'Malley
Who robbed the Cheyenne stage.

John D. Nesbitt

Way Out on the Elsinore Grand

On the summer-green plains of Montana
Where the eagle floats over the land,
'Neath the endless blue sky and soft sunshine
There's a place called the Elsinore Grand.

On the rangeland the shadows grow longer
As the cattle bed down for the night,
And the call of the coyote at sunset
Comes alive with the dying of light.

In a cabin alone on the prairie
When another day's work is all done,
There's a soft, golden glow in the window,
And a maiden who sits all alone.

I imagine her dressed in warm flannel
As she combs her dark hair in the light,
And I poke at the coals in my campfire
As I sit 'neath the heavens so bright.

And I plan how I'll get things in order
When my work is all done in the fall,
And I'll head my good cow pony northward
As I'm drawn by that long silent call.

Then I'll hear the sharp cry of the coyote
As I hear it in this lonesome land,
As I think of the girl who is waiting
Way out on the Elsinore Grand.

In the meanwhile I'll put by some money
For a ring that I saw in Cheyenne—
Just a thin band of gold with a diamond
That will shine on my sweet darling's hand.

THORNS ON THE ROSE

All my thoughts are of her in the distance,
As I work and save up as we planned
For the treasure of love that is waiting
Way out on the Elsinore Grand.

John D. Nesbitt

Jim Weston Isn't Dead

Was the talk throughout the bar-room
Where the worst of rumors spread
That a puncher from among us
Named Jim Weston was now dead.

'Twas the middle of November
When the roundup was all done,
All the steers were in the boxcars,
It was time to have some fun.

So our crew of twenty cowboys
Took a fast lope into town.
But we saw when we dismounted
That Jim Weston wasn't around.

"Now where the hell's he gone to?"
Asked his saddle pard named Max.
"I was sure he was among us
When we started makin' tracks."

No one had a ready answer
'Cept a man named Nat the Rat,
Who had never cinched a saddle,
Never worn a Stetson hat.

In the comfort of the bar-room
With a glass half-full of gin,
He was pleased to comment lightly
On the life of our pal Jim.

"Oh, he probably took a detour
So that he could get here first.
He most likely took a tumble
And is out there in the dirt.

THORNS ON THE ROSE

"That's the way with all these cowboys,
They can't wait to get to town,
So they ride hell-bent and reckless
Till their pony throws 'em down.

"So I wouldn't fret about it,
Save your tears, don't waste your breath,
'Cause if his neck ain't broken,
Then he's probably froze to death."

Well, the first to give rejoinder
Was our pal named Marble Mike.
He replied, "I don't think Weston's
Quite as dead as you would like."

"Oh, no one said he wished it,"
Answered Big Nose Pete the wit.
"But if Weston's dead, why doubt it?
There's no shame in sayin' it."

Then the next to speak was Johnny,
Who'd been Weston's pal for years.
He said, "Me 'n' Bob 'n' Dusty's
Got a hunch where Weston is."

"Weston's dead," said Pete the Parrot,
In refrain with Nat the Rat.
"But if *you* think you know different,
You can tell us where he's at."

Johnny poured a drink of whiskey,
Set his hat back on his head,
Looked around at his companions,
And to all who doubted said:

"Those of us that's ridden with him
Know Jim Weston isn't dead.
He's just holed up in his cabin
Snug and cozy in his bed,

"With a blonde-haired gal named Susie,
Who will keep him warm and fed.
So don't worry 'bout Jim Weston
'Cause he's nowhere close to dead."

Now you'd think that would have clinched it,
But the talk went on and on,
All about our friend Jim Weston
And if he was dead and gone.

As for me, I think Jim Weston
Is untouched by all this noise
And he wouldn't mind my singin'
'Long with Johnny and the boys:

"Those of us that's ridden with him
Know Jim Weston isn't dead.
He's just holed up in his cabin
Snug and cozy in his bed,

"With a blonde-haired gal named Susie,
Who will keep him warm and fed.
So don't worry 'bout Jim Weston
'Cause he's nowhere close to dead."

THORNS ON THE ROSE

Nebraska Girl

I've got a girl back in Nebraska
With sparkling eyes and long, dark hair—
A voice that rings with golden laughter,
And lips that brush away all care.

When last I saw her in Nebraska,
Beneath the spring-time moon so bright,
She whispered words demure and tender,
And held me in her arms so tight.

The golden moon above Nebraska
Lit up the prairie with its glow—
And showed to me a scene of wonder,
A dark-haired goddess here below.

I had to leave her in Nebraska—
But I'll go back when roundup's done,
And meet her on the golden prairie
Beneath the smiling autumn sun.

And when the winter in Nebraska
Gives way to prairie flowers in bloom,
We'll walk together, slow at sunset,
And watch the rising of the moon.

And when the moon above Nebraska
Lights up the evening warm and free,
We'll pledge our love in moonlit whispers,
My sweet Nebraska girl and me.

John D. Nesbitt

Please Come to Wyoming

Out on the wide prairie in broad sunny
    grasslands,
Or back in a canyon 'midst cottonwood trees,
Wherever the wildflowers bloom in the springtime,
You'll hear this sweet song on the soft evening
    breeze:

Yoodle-ooh, yoodle-ooh-hoo, so sings a lone
    cowboy,
Who with the wild roses wants you to be free.

This hand that I offer is yours now and always,
Please take it, my darling, step into the light;
The darkness and clouds you can leave there
    behind you
As forward you move into fields warm and bright.

Yoodle-ooh, yoodle-ooh-hoo, so sings a lone
    cowboy,
Who with the wild roses wants you to be free.

I offer you sunshine and flowers, my darling,
A few simple things from a country boy's world,
Please come to my arms now and let me protect
    you,
Please come to Wyoming to be my sweet girl.

Yoodle-ooh, yoodle-ooh-hoo, so sings a lone
    cowboy,
Who with the wild roses wants you to be free.

THORNS ON THE ROSE

We've seen how our lives have grown into each other,
We know that together we're destined to be,
So please let me help you ward off the dark shadows,
Please come to Wyoming, to sunlight and me.

Yoodle-ooh, yoodle-ooh-hoo, so sings a lone cowboy,
Who with the wild roses wants you to be free.

Out on the wide prairie in broad sunny grasslands,
Or back in a canyon 'midst cottonwood trees,
Wherever the wildflowers bloom in the springtime,
You'll hear this sweet song on the soft evening breeze:

Yoodle-ooh, yoodle-ooh-hoo, so sings a lone cowboy,
Who with the wild roses wants you to be free.

Yoodle-ooh, yoodle-ooh-hoo, so sings a lone cowboy,
Who with the wild roses wants you to be free.

Lonesome Jim

Sometimes he rides in on a sorrel,
Sometimes he shows up on a bay.
He drifts from one ranch to another
In wintertime when there's no pay.

He does any chore that the ranch cook
Or foreman will ask him to do—
Sort beans, fetch the water and firewood,
Or cut up some spuds for the stew.

He keeps to his bunk in the evening,
You won't hear him brag or complain,
Till one morning his bedroll has vanished,
And he's off on the grubline again.

To folks who don't know him he's a drifter
Who goes here and there on a whim,
But out on the range we don't judge him,
This fella we call Lonesome Jim.

Come springtime he rides for an outfit
And works for a dollar a day,
Rides outlaws and ropes like a top hand
And never has too much to say.

Then roundup is done, and this loner
Gets off of his stake rope a while,
Cuts loose like a wolf on a full moon,
Sings Mexican songs with a smile.

He tells of the woman who left him,
And a woman who died in the snow—
And he hopes he can find him another
Who'll stay for the end of the show.

THORNS ON THE ROSE

To folks who don't know him he's sorry,
A drunk from his spurs to his brim,
But out on the range we don't judge him,
This fella we call Lonesome Jim.

He drinks himself broke in November
Then lays up to get himself dry,
Goes back on the grubline for winter
With hopes that his hopes will not die.

We know him without ever knowing him,
We've seen it in others as well,
A man with a weakness that sometimes
He cannot control or dispel.

There's plenty of others who have it,
A weakness we're hard put to name—
It's not just for women or whiskey,
But it lives in the blood all the same.

To folks who don't know him he's a pity,
He'll never get straight or fit in,
But out on the range we don't judge him,
This fella we call Lonesome Jim.

No, out on the range we don't judge him,
We wish all the best luck to him—
For our own stories aren't all that different
From this fella we call Lonesome Jim.

Old Rope Corral

As I sit on a log at the edge of the fire
And another day comes to a close,
Far away from the laughter and gloom of the city,
Far away from the laurel and rose,

With the song of a stream as it chuckles in
    moonlight
Over secrets it never will tell,
I relax in the company of two faithful horses
Munching oats in the old rope corral.

It's a mighty fine camp in the heart of the
    mountains
Where I come when my time is my own,
Where the shuffle of hooves and the wind in the
    treetops
Knock the edge off of being alone.

As the fire burns down and the coals fall asunder,
There's a sight that I've come to know well—
A gash in the embers as bright as a blossom
Puts a glow on the old rope corral.

Though I'm far from the plains and the tents of
    the wicked
And the company of my fellow man,
Just the warmth of the fire on the brim of my
    Stetson
Lets me think of the times in Cheyenne

Where the love of a woman in cool dusky twilight
Gave me hopes that I cannot re-tell
Of a place and a time far away from my refuge
In a camp by an old rope corral.

THORNS ON THE ROSE

For we opened our hearts and discovered each
  other
And made plans for the future as well;
But the rules of life changed as she pledged to
  another,
And the curtain of solitude fell.

So I come to these mountains to stay with my
  horses
Where the water sings clear as a bell,
Where my tent stands in shadow in the pale
  mountain moonlight
In my camp by the old rope corral.

Well, the hope never dies that we'll find love again
Though the future we cannot foretell,
So we gather our strength as we take in the fire
Like the one by my old rope corral.

Rangeland Lament

Now he sleeps in the cold quiet grassland
Where he used to ride handsome and free,
Just a cowboy who worked for his wages
And on Sundays came calling for me.

Oh he called me his girl of the prairie,
And I called him my knight of the range.
And we fancied the call of the coyote—
Like our love, oh it never would change.

When we walked on the prairie in springtime
We would talk of the years yet to come—
How we'd save for a few head of cattle
And a homestead to call all our own.

We were married the fifth of November
When the wage-work was done for the fall,
And we filed for our land in December,
Plus a brand we could hang on the wall.

For the first year we scratched out a living,
Built a shack and a three-rail corral,
Put a dozen lean cows out to pasture
And were set when the first snowstorm fell.

Of the twelve cows we started in autumn
There were ten that had calves in the spring,
So we planned to have our first branding
When the grass was beginning to green.

But a cold rainy day in late April
Brought an end to the plans we had made
When a trio of men on dark horses
Arrived with the tools of their trade.

THORNS ON THE ROSE

From the cabin I heard the shots fired
And his voice as he called me in vain.
Three men in dark hats and dark slickers
Rode away in the cold April rain.

Now the months have gone by, and our cattle
Have been marked with a big outfit's brand,
And with each passing day it is harder
To believe in the justice of man.

When I hear the lone wail of the coyote
At the end of a short winter day
In the thin air of darkening rangeland,
Now his desolate notes seem to say:

Tell me who will mourn for a cowboy
As he sleeps 'neath the cold barren sod—
Tell me who will seek out his killers,
Tell me where is the justice of God?

Tell me who will mourn for a cowboy—
Tell me where is the justice of God?

Lone Winter

Now the wild geese of winter cross over my sky,
And the sun slips in scarlet as I watch the day die.
I stand at the doorway and look down the lane,
Where the dark ruts in twilight are all that
　　remain.

It's a cold world at nightfall as I step back inside,
Put a log on the embers where the fire has died,
Then return to the window to gaze out again
And remember the days that I waited in vain—

How the dreams died and withered, in the grip of
　　despair,
A shroud on the heart without candle or prayer—
For the desperate in love have no right to
　　complain
When there's ice on the doorstep and frost on the
　　pane.

Now the fire grows stronger and I shake off the
　　chill
That comes in the evening when all has gone still.
With the hearthfire and lamplight I once more
　　regain
The warmth that fled from me as I whispered her
　　name.

My blood's in December but it still has a trace
Of a pulse that once quickened in secret embrace,
And the blood can remember the fluting refrain
Of a meadowlark after a clean summer rain.

THORNS ON THE ROSE

Through the long night of winter, alone on the
 plain,
I feel the warmth seep into marrow and vein,
A soft flush of hope, given out by the flame,
Though there's ice on the doorstep and frost on
 the pane.

At the first break of morning I'll rise with the day
And gather my horses, the dun and the grey.
In a world dull as deer hide, the sun like a stain,
As the geese overhead stitch the sky with their
 skein,

I'll battle December with bridle and rein,
Forge one day to another like links in a chain.
If I fall from the saddle I will not complain
About ice on the doorstep and frost on the pane.

Traveler in the Snow

Well, we found her one cold Sunday morning
In the alley where hollyhocks grow.
'Neath the dead leaves and husks of last summer's
 stalks
Lay the woman who died in the snow.

She was wrapped in a coat and a blanket,
But the night had gone twenty below.
How she came to be there, to die all alone,
Was something we never would know.

For they come and they go on the train cars,
And they drop off in towns like our own.
They might stay for a day, and find nothing here,
Then they drift on to places unknown.

Oh, her face it was pale but not wrinkled,
Though her hair was beginning to grey.
And a necklace of gold, with a small garnet stone,
Cast a shine on a clear winter day.

For a moment, no more, she resembled
A person I'd known long ago.
Then the fancy passed on, and I saw as before
Just a woman who died in the snow.

Just a woman who died and was buried
At a stop on her journey alone.
Though we knew not her name, we laid her to rest
With her necklace and small garnet stone.

THORNS ON THE ROSE

Oh, they come and they go on the train cars
And they drop off in towns like our own.
They might stay for a day, and find nothing here,
Then they drift on to places unknown.

Blue Horse Mesa

Nate
They called me a rustler, I died in Wyoming,
My name on a blacklist by men who could pay.
I died on a hillside one cold day in April
When twenty-some gunmen sent bullets my way.

Lou Ellen
They called me unfaithful, I loved a range rider,
Up on a bright mesa beneath a blue sky.
But winter brought changes—a baby within me,
And cattlemen plotting for others to die.

Nate
Before the dark troubles with the cattlemen came,
A woman and I could say each other's name.

Lou Ellen
Before the dark fates and the killers would come,
My lover and I let our hearts beat as one

Both
When we met 'neath the sky at a place that was
  called
Blue Horse Mesa.

Lou Ellen
Now living in town, with a baby in blankets,
I thought of the man I could no longer see,
He rode the lone country from the Wall to the
    Mesa
From line camp to cow camp, without word from
    me.

THORNS ON THE ROSE

Nate
As bullets came thicker and evening drew closer,
I thought of the people I might never see—
My brother, my friends, and a woman now nameless,
Who up on a mesa shared moments with me.

Lou Ellen
*The blood in my veins told me something was wrong,
And deep to the marrow I felt hope was gone.*

Nate
*I knew that my chances were worn down and slim,
My hope running out and my time running thin.*

Both
*And our love like a dream in a place far away,
Blue Horse Mesa.*

Nate
They built up a fire, and smoke filled the cabin;
I had but one chance, and I'd give it a run.
I broke from the cabin, made thirty good paces,
Till the first bullets hit, and I knew I was done.

Lou Ellen
The news came on Monday, how Canton and Wolcott
With courage in numbers had gotten their man.
As I in my silence sat staring at nothing,
My journey of lone loveless sorrow began.

Nate
In the heart of lone country, out-gunned and out-manned,
I ran a lone race and I played a lone hand.

Lou Ellen
The cowards have left me alone with our son
To recall a brave man and our time in the sun.

Both
For we'll never in life meet again at our place,
Blue Horse Mesa.
No, we'll never in life meet again at that place,
Blue Horse Mesa.

THORNS ON THE ROSE

Don't Be a Stranger

Was in the early springtime
When the grass was showing green,
I met a girl in Hartville
On her way to Silver Springs.

With bright blue eyes that sparkled,
And long soft golden hair,
She told me of her father
And the ranch he had out there.

I told her I was headed
For a job some ways from her,
Out east of Rawhide Mountain,
Punchin' cows for the Single Spur.

Her sky-blue eyes they sparkled
As she tossed her hair and smiled,
Then touched my arm and murmured
In a voice so sweet and mild,

Darlin', don't be a stranger
When time is on your hands.
You're just one range over
In a large and lonesome land.

It takes a bit of courage
If you're a worthy man,
So don't be a stranger,
Come and see me when you can.

I worked those cows on roundup,
Finished up by mid-July,
Then turned my pony westward
To the girl with bright blue eyes.

John D. Nesbitt

Well the summer sky it sparkled,
And the meadowlarks sang true,
The lupine and the larkspur
And the flax all shining blue.

While crossin' Rawhide Mountain
On the ridges up on high,
I heard the wind a-whisperin'
With a murmur and a sigh.

The night grew dark and lonely,
As I heard the night bird sing
And recalled the voice so tender
Of the girl from Silver Springs.

Darlin', don't be a stranger
When time is on your hands.
You're just one range over
In a large and lonesome land.

It takes a bit of courage
If you're a worthy man,
So don't be a stranger,
Come and see me when you can.

On down the slope of Rawhide,
After riding two days straight,
I found the trail I needed,
And I tied up at her gate.

She seemed surprised to see me,
As a dark cloud crossed her face,
Then her smile came back like sunshine,
And she spoke with easy grace.

THORNS ON THE ROSE

She said she'd gotten married,
And was headed farther west.
It'd been so nice to know me,
And she wished me all the best.

As I stepped into the saddle
And rode back to the Single Spur,
Her early words still echoed,
And my mind was in a blur.

Darlin', don't be a stranger
When time is on your hands.
You're just one range over
In a large and lonesome land.

It takes a bit of courage
If you're a worthy man,
So don't be a stranger,
Come and see me when you can.

Now I ride the lonesome canyons
And the grasslands of this range,
It gives me time to ponder
Those ways that seem so strange.

I ride my horse in twilight
As the mournful night-owl sings,
And his voice recalls the soft words
Of the girl from Silver Springs.

I can't forget the sweetness
As her words run through my head,
And I think that at the moment
She had meant what she had said.

Her words, though false they've proven,
Have a calm effect on me,
For they help me see quite clearly
What was never meant to be.

Darlin', don't be a stranger
When time is on your hands.
You're just one range over
In a large and lonesome land.

It takes a bit of courage
If you're a worthy man,
So don't be a stranger,
Come and see me when you can.

THORNS ON THE ROSE

Great Lonesome

On the great lonesome plains of Wyoming
Where the winters last six months or more,
In a grave that is marked with wild roses
Lies a cowboy who died with his horse.

From the easy green pastures of summer
To the snow-crusted hard winter range,
With a horse and a song for companions,
Rode a puncher named Johnny Moraine.

In the country out north of Van Tassell
Lived a ranch girl that Johnny knew well.
She was sweet as cold water in August,
The raven-haired Josie O'Dell.

It was thirteen long miles from the bunkhouse
To the homestead where Josie's light burned.
Leaving early on cold winter Sundays,
By moonlight he made his return.

On a cold day in middle December,
For winter came early that fall,
He picked out his best red bandana
And took his wool chaps from the wall.

With the lariat of rawhide he'd braided,
And a hatband of horsehair he wove,
He whistled a tune to the buckskin
As out of the ranch yard he rode.

At a frost-covered pane in the bunkhouse
Stood a man who had hate in his heart.
He scratched with his thumb for a peep-hole
As he watched the young cowboy depart.

How deep runs the malice in some men
Over things that will never be theirs,
For this puncher he had a sick fancy
For the girl with the raven-dark hair.

When Johnny left Josie's that evening
As the moon was beginning to rise
And reflected on snow that had fallen,
He could see all the stars in the sky.

He found the trail easy to follow
For the night was as clear as the day,
So his thoughts drifted back to the ranch house
As homeward he traveled his way.

He went down through a draw where he startled
An owl from its perch in a tree,
With the branches so stark in the moonlight
Every twig and small fork he could see.

Through the cold, thin air of the rangeland
Came the blast of a gun loud and clear.
As the buckskin horse shuddered and crumpled,
The rider jumped into the clear.

But a second shot ripped from the rifle,
Sending Johnny face-down in the snow.
Then the silence returned as the moonlight
Spread over the still forms below.

In the morning the other hands found him,
With his angora chaps stained in red,
And his arm draped over the buckskin
On a blanket of snow for their bed.

THORNS ON THE ROSE

Well, the puncher named Cline was among them
When they brought Johnny back to the Node.
And they buried him there on a hillside
Overlooking the range that he rode.

Now the killer could not dare to court her,
For he lived every day with his fear,
While she planted wild roses on the hillside
And watered them all through the year.

And he might have gone on for a long while,
As he peeped out at life through the pane,
But a rider came down from Montana,
And he said that his name was Moraine.

And in less than a week from a trestle
Overlooking an old silver mine
At the end of a rope was found dangling
The remains of a puncher named Cline.

Then the brother went back to Montana,
And Josie at length settled down
With a rancher not far from Van Tassell
And the grave where they laid Johnny down.

Now they say on a clear night in winter
When the moonlight shines down with its glow,
There's a spirit comes drifting in silence
Wearing chaps that are white as the snow.

Thorns on the Rose

A flaxen-haired maiden from Sweden
Stepped down from the train in Cheyenne.
She said, "I'm a wheat farmer's sweetheart.
I've come here to marry my man.

"I love him though I've never met him,
His photograph I've never seen—
But here I am now in this city,
To be his sweet bride at sixteen.

"He's written me long, lovely letters
About the big farm he has here—
One hundred and six-ty acres,
And six months' vacation each year.

"He tells me I'll find it delightful
Where winters are generally warm—
So please, if you can, won't you tell me
The way to the Johnson farm?"

Well, the man she addressed was a cowboy
Who'd just ridden in from the range.
He said, "If it's Johnsons you're seekin',
There's a hundred from here to LaGrange.

"Them and their cousins, the Nelsons,
They came out in droves from the East.
They're scattered all over the prairie,
And plowin' it up to grow wheat.

"Not one out of ten has a woman,
So lonesome it is in this land,
That long, lovely letters get written
To make the adventure seem grand.

THORNS ON THE ROSE

"You're young and you're sweet and you're pretty,
And I hope you don't think I'm unkind,
But a maiden like you deserves warning,
Before she walks into things blind.

"That six-month vacation you mentioned
Will be spent in the ice and the snow,
Knockin' mud off the toes of the chickens,
Milkin' cows when it's forty below.

"The other six months aren't much better
With the wind and the dust and the heat,
Then a dark cloud that comes out of nowhere,
With a hailstorm to flatten the wheat.

"On Monday you wash clothes for the baby,
On Tuesdays you scrub and you bake,
On Wednesdays dig spuds in the garden
And keep an eye out for the snake."

"Enough!" said the maiden, now blushing,
"You're making me feel like a child.
Is there nothing out here in this country
To make all the hardship worthwhile?

"If you weren't such a clear-eyed young fellow
I'd think you were telling me this
To make me forget about Johnson
And his promise of marital bliss.

"So tell me, young man, on your honor,
What better things you can propose—
Is yours a soft life of warm sunshine
Where harm never comes to the rose?"

John D. Nesbitt

"Oh, no," said the cowboy, still smiling,
"The only rose I know is wild.
It blooms for a few days in springtime
When the weather is fragile and mild.

"But the petals soon blemish and wither,
And the rosebush goes back to the thorn.
So my life is not one to entice you
And I fear it would make you forlorn.

"But there's one thing I have over Johnson,
I can tell by the look in your eye—
You don't mind a straight-talkin' cowboy
Who can't find it in him to lie.

"And at least you know what I look like—
You don't seem repulsed by the clothes
Of an honest range-ridin' cowpuncher
Who admits there are thorns on the rose."

"That's true," said the flaxen-haired maiden,
"You seem to be honest and kind.
But a young girl has got to be careful
With someone she meets the first time."

"It's all for the best," said the puncher,
"To not take a step you'll regret,
And I hope you're convinced not to marry
This wheat-farmer you've never met.

"And if you don't mind, I'll invite you
In the light of this warm afternoon,
To stroll through the cactus and sagebrush,
And see the wild roses in bloom."

THORNS ON THE ROSE

So off went the flaxen-haired maiden
To stroll arm-in-arm with this man,
As meadowlarks sang to the whistle
Of the train pulling out of Cheyenne.

If ever this story has a moral,
It might go like this, I suppose:
Don't promise your love to a stranger,
But don't fear the thorns on the rose.

Don't promise your love to a stranger,
But don't fear the thorns on the rose.

John D. Nesbitt

Angelique; or, A Lover's Quest

I've been west to California,
I've been north to Idaho,
I've been east to old Virginia,
I've been south to Mexico.

But of all the spots I've been to
There's a place I love the best,
In the heart of the Rocky Mountains,
In the distant cold northwest.

'Neath the sky of old Montana,
On the banks of Powder Creek,
Lives a brave and honest trapper
With his daughter Angelique.

She has cheeks as white as ivory,
Framed in silky long black hair,
And her eyes are blue as lupine
That adorns the meadows there.

Across the valley is my cabin,
Just a humble twelve-by-ten,
Where I hope to hang my saddle
When my pony sheds again.

It was on a bright May morning
That I kissed her on the cheek
And with many a tear and promise
Took my leave of Angelique.

Safe inside an empty watch-case
In the pocket of my vest
Was a lock of hair she gave me,
In response to my request—

THORNS ON THE ROSE

For not once in eighteen summers
On the banks of Powder Creek
Had a person with a camera
Photographed my Angelique.

Nor had any other artist
Ever drawn or painted her—
Never brushed her hair on canvas,
Never sketched her smile demure.

Thus inside my golden watch case
Tied in thread and wrapped with care
Was my version of a portrait
In a lock of raven hair.

And I told her as I kissed her
That when once my furs were sold,
I would pledge her my devotion
With a diamond set in gold.

Raven hair in a golden case
To remind me of a place
A dark-haired girl with wistful face,
Lingering tears and soft embrace.
Like a tiny treasure chest
Tucked away inside my vest
To put lonesome fears to rest,
It went with me on my quest.

Then we said good-bye that morning
And I left her all alone,
As I led the pack mules eastward
To the banks of the Yellowstone,

John D. Nesbitt

Where I trailed along the river
'Midst the herds of buffalo
And cut east towards Dakota
Through the land of the Sioux and Crow.

At the campfire every evening
'Neath the silver stars of night
I recalled my blue-eyed darling
With her blushing cheeks of white.

And as if to see her picture,
With a motion soft as prayer,
I would open up the watch-case
To behold her beauty there.

Then beneath the starry heavens
I would lay me down to rest,
There to dream of one girl only
Who was waiting in the west.

Each new dawn would find me stirring,
Loading up the mules again,
To resume my travel eastward
On across the endless plain.

Then I crossed the famous Badlands,
Where the coyotes wailed at night,
And the buzzards wheeled in circles
In the sky so vast and bright.

Oh, it made a man feel little
In a land so vast and spare,
And I prayed to God in heaven
Not to let me perish there—

THORNS ON THE ROSE

But to help me cross the Badlands
And escape the vulture's beak,
So that I might sell my plunder
And return to Powder Creek

Raven hair in a golden case
To remind me of a place
A dark-haired girl with wistful face,
Lingering tears and soft embrace.
Like a tiny treasure chest
Tucked away inside my vest
As a token of the best,
It kept me steady on my quest.

But before I left the Badlands,
On a warm and breathless day,
I observed another horseman
Who was headed north my way.

He came riding from the Badlands
On a horse as black as coal,
Like a skiff upon the ocean
As the waves beneath it roll—

For the billows of the prairie
Seemed to move beneath the shape
Of the loping mounted horseman
In his flowing dusky cape.

He had silver spurs that jingled
And a flat-crowned charcoal hat;
The pearl handle on his six-gun
Matched the pin on his cravat.

John D. Nesbitt

He had one continuous eyebrow
And a pair of gimlet eyes,
But a smile so warm and friendly
That it took me by surprise.

My new friend fell in beside me
With the jingle of his spurs
As I led my pack mules onward
With my winter's catch of furs.

For three nights we camped together,
Shared a fire upon the trail,
Rolled our blankets out like brothers,
With no hint of his betrayal.

Then upon the third bleak morning
As I rose to greet the day,
He was gone like cold grey ashes
That the wind has swept away.

He was gone with horse and bedroll,
By the dawn's first rosy streak,
And my blood ran cold as water
As I thought of Angelique—

For the night before, at moonrise
As I settled down to rest,
I had folded up my clothing
And on top had put my vest.

Now the early daylight showed me
Where this thief had made his play—
He had pillaged my gold watch-case
From my waistcoat where it lay.

THORNS ON THE ROSE

No doubt thinking it had value,
For it looked like an antique,
He had robbed me of my treasure—
He had stolen Angelique.

Raven hair in a golden case
To remind me of a place
A dark-haired girl with wistful face,
Lingering tears and soft embrace.
Like a serpent in the nest,
Tainted fingers of a guest
Took the treasure from my vest
And changed the nature of my quest.

Now the smold'ring hate within me
Leapt ablaze like burning pitch,
And the only thought I nurtured
Was to kill that son of a b----.

But before I could get vengeance
I would have to sell my furs,
To have money and provisions
As I tracked those silver spurs.

I made haste from that day onward,
By the light of sun and moon,
Till I reached the broad Missouri
On the fifteenth day of June.

First I sold my pile of beaver
Then the mules and all the gear,
Filled my warbag with provisions
And then headed north to Pierre.

John D. Nesbitt

All along the trail I questioned
Every man I chanced upon,
And the answers pointed northward
As I learned where he had gone.

Through that rough Dakota country
Night and day I traced his route,
Till I lost his trail completely
At a place called Thunder Butte.

On a hunch I headed southward,
Always looking for my man,
Till another fortnight brought me
To the cowtown called Cheyenne.

There as always I asked questions,
And at length to my surprise
I was told about a stranger
With a pair of gimlet eyes.

Yes, his silver spurs did jingle,
And he wore a charcoal hat,
And the handle of his six-gun
Matched the pearl on his cravat.

In Cheyenne he was remembered
Though he stayed for just one day,
And he said he soon expected
To go back to Santa Fe.

Raven hair in a golden case
To remind me of a place
A dark-haired girl with wistful face,
Lingering tears and soft embrace.

THORNS ON THE ROSE

Now the burning in my chest
Kept me onward pushed and pressed,
So consumed now with my quest
That I could not stop for rest.

Down through Denver, then, I tracked him,
Always dreaming of the day
I would come upon this scoundrel
And at last would make him pay.

But my dreams remained elusive,
For pursue him as I might,
He was like a fleeting shadow,
Out of reach and out of sight.

So the summer slipped to autumn
As I clung to my belief
That the trail ahead would shorten
As I stalked this phantom thief.

But the tracks were always faded,
And the campfire coals were dead,
And no matter how I hurried,
He remained one camp ahead.

Now his trail leads through the mountains
To the west of Santa Fe,
And the sun is slipping southward
With the dying of each day.

And my horse's coat grows thicker
As the days grow short and cold,
And my rifle seems so heavy
And the reins so hard to hold.

John D. Nesbitt

As the soft white snow comes falling
I can feel it on my cheek,
And it takes me back in memory
To the banks of Powder Creek.

But the sullen hope within me
Drives me daily on my way
To seek justice for a girl who
Lives a thousand miles away.

Raven hair in a golden case
To remind me of a place
A dark-haired girl with wistful face,
Lingering tears and soft embrace,
Gone so long now from my vest.
Though I yearn to take a rest,
The hollow burning in my chest
Pushes me upon my quest—

Pushes me upon my quest—
Through the mountains to the west,
Where I have but one request:
Give me justice and then rest.

Acknowledgements

"Like All the Others," *What It Can't Save* (Columbus, Ohio: Pudding Magazine and Publications, 1986). Also in *Wide Open Magazine*, October 1986.

"Wild Rose of Wyoming," *Wyoming: The Hub of the Wheel*, no. 4 (1987).

"Labor of Love," *Wide Open Magazine*, Fall 1987.

"I Won't Live in L.A.," *Wyoming: The Hub of the Wheel*, no. 7 (1990).

"I Planted Apple Trees," "To Officer Miller," "A Son and a Father," *The Dakotah*, Fall 1991.

"In the Broncho Bar," "Friday's Impression," "When Life Is Better Than a Good Cowboy Song," *The Dakotah*, Fall 1992.

"Dark House, Dark Lady," *Wyoming: The Hub of the Wheel*, no. 8 (1992).

"When Life is Better Than a Good Cowboy Song," "Early Spring Ride," *Visions of Wyoming*, ed. Marik Turbes (Casper: Star Tribune Publications, 1993).

"I Held It All Together For So Long," "Some Things I Kept," *The Dakotah*, Fall 1993.

"Palenque Chihuahua," *The Dakotah*, 1994-95.

"Under Cloak of Night," *Emerging Voices*, Spring 1999.

"To the North of Old Cheyenne," "Down in Santa Fe," and an earlier version of "Angelique; or, a Lover's Quest," *Adventures of the Ramrod Rider* (Casper: Endeavor Books, 1999).

"Roasting a Goose," *Man from Wolf River* (NY: Leisure Books, 2001).

"Nebraska Girl," *Emerging Voices*, Spring 2001. Also in *For the Norden Boys* (NY: Leisure Books, 2002) and *Wyoming's Cowboy Poets* (Evansville: Medallion Books, 2004).

"Please Come to Wyoming," *Black Hat Butte* (NY: Leisure Books, 2003). Also in *Wyoming's Cowboy Poets* (Evansville: Medallion Books, 2004).

"Lone Winter," *Emerging Voices*, Spring 2005. Also in *Lonesome Range* (NY: Leisure Books, 2006).

"Lonesome Jim," "Blue Horse Mesa," *Emerging Voices*, Spring 2007. "Lonesome Jim" also in *Stranger in Thunder Basin* (NY: Leisure Books, 2009).

"Doing Better,"*WyoPoets Newsletter*, January 2008.

"Thorns on the Rose," *Emerging Voices*, Spring 2008. Also in *Trouble at the Redstone* (NY: Leisure Books, 2008).

"Old Rope Corral," *Emerging Voices*, Spring 2009. Also in *Gather My Horses* (NY: Leisure Books, 2011).

The first edition of *Thorns on the Rose* was published by Western Trail Blazer in 2013 and won a Will Rogers Medallion Award, Third place, for poetry

THORNS ON THE ROSE

in 2014.

"Jim Weston Isn't Dead," *Dark Prairie*, (Waterville, ME: Five Star Publishing, 2013).

"Jack O'Malley," *Across the Cheyenne River* (Waterville, ME: Five Star Publishing, 2014).

"Don't Be a Stranger," *Don't Be a Stranger* (Waterville, ME: Five Star Publishing, 2015).

"Rangeland Lament," *Emerging Voices*, Spring 2014. Also in *Death in Cantera* (Waterville, ME: Five Star Publishing, 2016)

"Till the Death of My Honky-Tonk Heart," *Emerging Voices*, Spring 2014. Also in *Blue Springs* (Azle, TX: Fire Star Press, 2017)

"Way Out on the Elsinore Grand," *Destiny at Dry Camp* (Waterville, ME: Five Star Publishing, 2017).

"Prairie Center," *Saddlebag Dispatches*, Autumn/Winter 2018. This poem also won the Western Writers of America Spur Award for Best Poem in 2019.

"Traveler in the Snow," *Dusk Along the Niobrara* (Waterville, ME: Five Star Publishing, 2019).

About the Author

John D. Nesbitt lives in the plains country of Wyoming, where he teaches English and Spanish at Eastern Wyoming College. His articles, reviews, fiction, and poetry have appeared in numerous magazines and anthologies. He is best known as a fiction writer, with more than thirty-five books of traditional western, contemporary, mystery, and retro/noir fiction.

THORNS ON THE ROSE

John has won many awards for his work, including two awards from the Wyoming State Historical Society (for fiction), two awards from Wyoming Writers for encouragement of other writers and service to the organization, two Wyoming Arts Council literary fellowships (one for fiction, one for non- fiction), a Western Writers of America Spur finalist award for his western novel *Raven Springs*, and the Spur award itself for his noir short story "At the End of the Orchard," for his western novels *Trouble at the Redstone* and *Stranger in Thunder Basin*, and for his poem "Prairie Center."

For more information about John D. Nesbitt and his books and poetry, please visit him at:

http://www.johndnesbitt.com

Made in the USA
Lexington, KY
09 April 2019